* With Face to the Wall

* * * * * * * * * * *

WITH FACE TO THE WALL

Selected Poems of MILTOS SAHTOURIS

Translation and Introduction by
Kimon Friar

Washington,
The Charioteer Press
1968

THIS IS A *Charioteer Book.*

Published by The Charioteer Press, 601 19th Street, N.W., Washington, D.C. 20006.

Manufactured in the United States of America.

FIRST EDITION LIMITED TO 300 COPIES.

ACKNOWLEDGMENTS

Some of these translations have appeared in *Athene*, *Modern European Poetry* (Bantam Books, 1966), *Poetry*, *Shenandoah*. The author makes grateful acknowledgment to the editors.

CONTENTS

CONTENTS

INTRODUCTION

Míltos (Miltiades) Sahtoúris was born on July 29, 1919, and regards as his place of origin the illustrious island of Hydra, where his great, great grandfather made his place in history among the admirals of the Greek fleet who fought the Turks during the Greek War of Independence. Though in his early years he endured the formal training and routine observances of Athenian youth, and even completed his studies in law at the University of Athens, he never troubled to take his degree. A tall, burly man of athletic build but with eyes agitated with the pale cast of thought (somewhat reminiscent of the stature and sensitivity of Theodore Roethke), he saluted the heroism and enterprise of his stalwart ancestors, then resolutely turned his back on all the world of affairs, public studies, business and social amenities. Living on an extremely small income, he disappeared into an inner world of his own, one of remarkable consistency. He has never traveled beyond the boundaries of Greece and has even turned his back on the notorious beauty of the Greek mainland and its myriad islands. Even in Athens, which he rarely leaves, he restricts himself to the confines of his neighborhood and a small group of friends and relatives.

From this private country Sahtoúris sends us the image-laden and blood-splattered reports of an explorer from what seems at first to be another planet. At times they read like the reports of a missionary, a doctor, a diagnostician, an aeronaut, a saviour, and at times like the cryptic declarations of a Cumaean Sybil, the mad but prophetic utterances of a Cassandra. It is from all these, arranged in chronological order, that I have chosen, icon after icon, the strange, obsessed, neurotic, yet nostalgic poems of Míltos Sahtoúris, which, we begin to realize, reflect our own world like underwater traceries of our most familiar objects: *The Forgotten Woman*, 1945; *Ballads*, 1948; *With Face to the Wall*, 1952; *When I Speak To You*, 1956; *The Phantoms* or *Joy in the Other Street*, 1958; *The Stroll*, 1960; *The Stigmata*, 1962; *The Seal* or *The Eighth Moon*, 1964.

Perhaps the title of his third book best describes the stance and perspective that Míltos Sahtoúris has taken: *With Face to the Wall*. His rigidity in that position is suggestive of many causes and many effects. It is that of a small child who has been placed in a corner facing a wall by parent or teacher. He stands there, not quite understanding why he is being punished, but beginning to feel, as time lapses into time, that he must indeed have been guilty of some great sin, some unspeakable crime. The only recourse of the child is to shut his eyes tight and fly off into a world of his own fantastic compensation. It is also a position taken on his own volition by a man in early youth who deliberately turns his back on the world that he may gaze into it more piercingly. The wall on which he now stares with a third, inner, eye, is that which separates lover from lover, husband from wife, friend from friend, nation from nation, no matter of what material it is composed: iron, bamboo, silk, stone, invisible glass, or yielding air. It is at once barrier and barricade, stronghold and iron cage, prison and asylum wall. It is the Wailing Wall where every minority group—and whose numbers are more depleted than those of the true poets?—bewails its fate and thus the fate of all individuals and of all nations. And it is finally that wall in Greece during the German-Italian Occupation of the early 1940's against which—as against all similar walls throughout the world—men, women, and children, poets among them (as in Spain), were ruthlessly propped up as hostages and shot down by rifle or machinegun fire. It is a nightmare world of Hitler and Hiroshima that makes the distorted and dislocated images of Sahtoúris seem but pale depictions of actual events. He belongs to the postwar generation of poets who had seen the whitewashed walls of Greece suddenly splattered red, and all his poetry has been colored by this terror, recorded particularly in such poems as "Nightmare," "He Is Not Oedipus," and "Death." History is forever brutally repeating itself: Aegisthus and Orestes become equated with Kostas and Alexis, Oedipus with Elias the grocer, the descent of the Virgin Mary with the ascent of Achilles' horses, hand grenades with bitter oranges. As in *Macbeth*, one word colors all of his poetry: blood.

It would be correct to say that Sahtoúris did not at first choose of his own free will to stand with his face to the wall. Like most of us during the past two generations, he was placed there first by parent, priest, or teacher for punishment, or out of original sin, then by the enemy, and finally by some Kafkaesque tribunal of the universe, unknown and mysterious. It was only later that he recognized his personal wounds as the stigmata of the entire world's guilt. Like Maria, in the poem by that name, when everyone began to speak through him unbearably, as through a medium, he took refuge by beginning to fly in imagination round and round a room that was both prison and escape, for, as he writes in "The Saviour," "every room is an open wound." He is obsessed with disease, and his creatures are as stigmatized as Grünewald's Christ and demons in the Isenheim altarpiece. "And if I should find the pharmacy closed," he cries out, "and if I should find the pharmacist dead, and if I should find my heart displayed in the pharmacy window?" In his early verses image follows image without logical intent, as in the naturally surrealist world of childhood, evoking, in their totality, worlds of alienation, agony, lost innocence, love betrayed, fear, anxiety, guilt. It would be futile in many of these poems, and in the whole of Sahtoúris' work, to attempt any thoroughly logical deduction or sequential exegesis. "My poetry is many things which elude me," he once told me, "and which I do not understand. And if I did understand, I would not wish to reveal it."

The mature poet opened his eyes and gazed intently on the mottled wall before him. From its patterns formed by rain, mold, decay, moss, blood, and sunstains, and from his remembrance of the world behind him, he constructed a mirror-world of his own. "Poetry, without my being aware of it," Sahtoúris told me, "was like a mirror of my inner self, and behold, I held in my hands another mirror in which everything I saw was reflected. I shattered both mirrors, and from the splintered crystals built my own Orpheus-mirror in which true poetry stands revealed, my own life." A wall gazed at so intently, so persistently, so obsessively does indeed become a reflective image, a hallucination, a water-mirror into which Narcissus may drown, or a shield-mirror where Perseus may slay the monster

Medusa of form by subtle indirection. In this world of inverted images, girls fall on their backs and spit on their dreams, a dog drinks up his tears on the ground, lovers carve trees on their hearts, plates break as soon as they are touched, kisses open and close on the floor, moons are knifed, a kneeling horse eats up the floor boards, saints run in the streets, and bats fly like sorrowful gospels.

Like most poets who in childhood fled into a world fantastically yet naturally their own, Sahtoúris later in early youth grasped gratefully and deliberately at the techniques of surrealism to depict a world of images that had an irrational logic of their own. But when he tried to pierce through his enclosures and into the world beyond and behind, his poems became increasingly lyrical and dramatic. Without abandoning the dislocated imagery of surrealism, which after all coincides with his own natural view of the world, he found that his images began to convey an immediately apprehensible picturization of the world's own dislocations, and it is his images, almost alone, that contain the full burden of Sahtoúris' vision. His poems are almost all very short, written in free verse without rhyme, and in brief declarative or interrogative sentences with the simplest diction and syntax. They reveal a strangely silent world, like that of Chirico, like that of old cinematic films, like that of Picasso's "Guernica," and though there is often a sudden cry of agony—a dog or a dove or a virgin howls—we look into mouths that are gaping wounds without sound. In this world of alienation Sahtoúris lives. When his friends stray into another room, it is as though he has lost them forever. And love is the most shattering experience of all, filled with erotic obsessions, forever found and forever lost, a heavy sickness: lovers are puppets pushed, not pulled, by strings. "My poetry is fundamentally erotic," Sahtoúris once said many years ago. "It is composed of two bodies that embrace until suddenly they discover that their faces are black and besmirched with blood."

Yet no man, no poet, pushed to such extremity, has not been impelled there by an inordinate love of the world, of all animate and inanimate things. Sahtoúris' agony is not that of illusion, but of disillusion, horror at the brutality of a world a thousandfold more surrealist than his own. Occasionally, therefore, he celebrates what must have been the pristine innocence of childhood and the world, what man and the world may one day still hopefully become. His belief is that poetry, no matter how shattering, may transform tragedy by shaping it into the ordered beauty of image and cadence. He sprinkles ugliness with beauty, casts a rainbow spray of colors among his gaping images, wants every spring to be judged by its own gladness, nails us to the pavement that we may admire the celestial advertisements, transforms mundane reality into cinematic art that defies death until one day, he declares, we may "pass through the black burning hole of the sun." In "The Poet," Sahtoúris has written his own epitaph: a white bird shall recite his verses in a frightening darkness, but where, as in "Threnody," butterflies will strike back at knives and the night shall become as beautiful as day.

KIMON FRIAR

* With Face to the Wall

BEAUTY

He sprinkled ugliness with beauty
he took a guitar
he walked along a riverbank
singing

He lost his voice
the delirious lady stole it
who cut off her head amid the crimson waters
and the poor man no longer has a voice with which to sing
and the river rolls
the tranquil head with its closed eyelashes

Singing

THE DREAM

Notre voyage à nous est entièrement imaginaire. Voilà sa force.
—L. F. CELINE

The everliving dream
caresses its white hair

Boys undress in the light
throw the ball and shout in triumph
a Frankish priest with his finger points at Lycabbetos
a naked boy smiles at the girls
they grow tall in their branches they shout
he is crippled he is crippled
afterwards they plunge with shame in the red water

Young women undress in the shadows
in the endless harbors frightened,
a surgeon on the balcony opens and closes his lancets
tired stevedores lie in wait
to cut the ship's cables
to tear the virginal dresses in tatters
to mutiny and hang the captain
on the large mast of the sky
for women to clench their fingers
to close their eyes to sigh
to show their teeth their tongues

The voyage of joy begins

The sorrowful woman undressed in the dark
she clambered up the wretched house
and stopped the futile music
she laughed at the mirror lifted her hands
painted her face with the color
of an expectation saw the sun
on her watch and then remembered:

"Look, the poem has come true
but the illegitimate boy and the color
make a gift of joy
and how can they photograph this place
it is a place of hypocrisy
it is a land where boys
who have lost their innocence lie in ambush
and spread out their hands to the open window
that the sick kisses might fall
that the young short-lived orphans
might fall weeping from the windows
squeezing in their wounded hands
a tuft of white hair

From a very ancient dream"

THE THREE LOVERS

On the rain-soaked roads of evening
rises a haze of seablue light
a broad heart on each heart
and with ruinous footsteps
three lovers hand in hand go by
the first

Hangs his love on a tree
and prays beneath the tree at midnight
for his love to descend clinging to the leaves
for the flood of melting leaves to cease
a dog drinks up his tears on the ground
and love amidst the branches stones him
the tree howls the wind the dog
the second

Gave his love away to a crazy violinist
the crazy man composed a song about her
the sky rains down flowers coins
the roads resound with the fatal violin
all have now learned the song of love
with bluecold puckered lips they whistle it
but only he does not know it
the third

Made a boat out of his love
and launched it on the three seas
he has become a boy again
and builds castles of sand
he gathers shells pebbles
and waits for his boat for love
to return again

All three have carved a tree on their hearts
a violin played close to the ear will drive them crazy
and in the underseas the captain plays with coral

THE SAVIOUR

I count on the fingers of my severed hands
the hours in which I have strayed in these rooms of the
wind
I do not have other hands my beloved and the doors
will not close and the days are unyielding

With my bare feet I splash about in these dirty waters
with my bare heart I search for (but not for myself)
a skyblue window
how did they ever build so many rooms so many tragic
books
without a crack of light
without a breath of oxygen
for the sick reader

Since every room is also an open wound
how shall I descend the crumbling stairs again
to bring through mud and wild dogs
bandages of rose and medicines
and if I should find the pharmacy closed
and if I should find the pharmacist dead
and if I should find my heart displayed in the pharmacy
window

No no it is ended there is no salvation

The rooms shall remain as they are
with the wind and the reeds of the wind
with splinters of glass faces that groan
with their colorless bleeding
with porcelain hands that stretch out toward me
with unpardonable oblivion

My own severed and *fleshly* hands were forgotten
that very moment when I was counting up their agony

OBSERVATORY

Burglars of the sun
they had never seen a green twig
they had never touched a burning mouth
they do not know what the color of the sky is

In darkened rooms locked up
they do not know if they will die
they lurk in ambush
with black masks with heavy telescopes
with stars in their pockets dirty with crumbs
with stones of cowards in their hands
they lurk in other planets for the light

Let them die

Let every spring be judged by its gladness
by its color every single flower
by its caress every single hand
by its trembling every single kiss

NIGHTMARE

Her name was *Seashore* and *Sunday*. She had black eyes black hair black garments black petticoats and a pure black horse. But they called her *Seashore* and *Sunday*. Her house was on an island and it was full of pistols crimson robes flags netted stars machine guns diving helmets hooks chests with dreams and chests with bullets island dresses lamps with colored glasses colored handkerchiefs and an old rusted cannon. As night fell she would light a lantern in the window. It would flare up—go out flare up—go out and immediately a desolate boat would anchor by the side of the iron door of the house and one by one five men would glide into the house. In a little while from a secret small door covered by cactus the First Man emerged dead. The Second with his face splattered with blood held a very beautiful infant in his arms. The Third also splattered with blood held an automatic rifle in his arms. The Fourth dragged himself along wrapped from top to toe in a heavy dark green material. The Fifth was dead also. But the most beautiful dead person was the girl in her pure white dress lying on the floor in the middle of the room by the side of her slain black horse she also splattered with blood her hands crossed high on her breast with a smile and with a green twig in her mouth while the five Germans weak before her saluted at attention.

DEATH

No one killed this particular man
he was not the harbor watchman
he was not a warrior in battle
in trains he would bring animals in iron cages
and his heart nested on the high mountains
some time or other his blood will speak
and then small black birds shall smother the clouds
bearded black winds shall encircle the fields
pear trees shall sing his history
in the house of flame with the wild animals
the cups of death upon the table
the sunless curtains the flint the cold words
flint and cold kisses without love
with the wanton girls of silence
who every evening would close the windows
who every evening would crucify sleep
who every evening would tear up and eat their dresses
they would fall on their backs and spit on their dreams

THE GIFTS

Today I wore a
warm red blood
today men love me
a woman smiled at me
a girl gave me a seashell
a boy gave me a hammer

Today I kneel on the sidewalk
and nail the naked feet of the passers-by
to the pavement tiles
they are all in tears
but no one is frightened
all remain in the places to which I had come in time
they are all in tears
but they gaze at the celestial advertisements
and at a beggar who sells hot cross buns
in the sky

Two men whisper
what is he doing is he nailing our hearts?

yes he is nailing our hearts

well then he is a poet

DEEP MINE

I write you filled with fear from a nocturnal arcade
lit by a lamp as small as a thimble
a wagon carefully passes above me
it gropes its distances not to hit me
but I pretend sometimes to be sleeping sometimes
to be darning a pair of old stockings
because all things about me have become strangely worn
out

At home
yesterday
as I opened the wardrobe it vanished it became
dust together with all its clothing
the plates break as soon as they are touched
I am afraid and have hidden the knives and forks
my hair has become somewhat like cotton batting
my mouth has turned white and it hurts me
my hands are stone
my feet are wooden
three small children scurry about me crying
I do not know how this happened and they call me
Mother

I wanted to write you of our old happiness
but I have forgotten how to write of happy things
R e m e m b e r   m e

HE IS NOT OEDIPUS

A huge sky filled with swallows
enormous halls doric columns
the hungry ghosts
sitting in chairs in the corners
weeping
the rooms with dead birds
Aegisthus the fishing net Kostas
Kostas the fisherman the afflicted
a room filled with tulles of many colors that flutter in the
    wind
bitter-oranges break the windowpanes
and enter
Kostas killed
Orestes killed
Alexis killed
break the chains on the windows
and enter
Kostas Orestes Alexis
others return to the streets from the fiesta
with lights with flags with trees
they call on Maria to descend
they call on Maria to descend from Heaven
the horses of Achilles fly in the heavens
rockets attend their flight
the sun rolls down from hill to hill
and the moon is a green lantern
filled with alcohol
then silence brings night to the streets

and the blind man comes out with his cane
children follow him on tiptoe
he is not Oedipus
he is Elias from the vegetable market
he plays an exhausting and fatal flute
he is dead Elias from the vegetable market

THE SKY

Birds, black arrows of difficult sorrow
it is not easy for you to love the sky
many of you have learned to say it is blue
do you not know its caves its forests its rocks?
As you are passing thus like winged whistles
you tear your flesh on its windowpanes
your downy feathers are glued to its heart

And when night comes from the trees fearfully
you look at its white handkerchief, the moon
at the naked virgin who howls in its lap
at the mouth of the old lady with her rotted teeth
at the stars with swords and golden strings
at its lightning its thunder its rain
at the distant sensual pleasure of its galaxy

ON THE NATURE OF THE BEAST

Do not go away beast
beast with the iron teeth
I shall build you a wooden house
I shall give you an earthen jug
I shall also give you a spear
I shall also give you more blood to play with

I shall bring you to other harbors
to see how ships devour their anchors
how masts break in two
and how flags are suddenly painted black

I shall find for you the same girl again
who at night will tremble bound in the dark
I shall find for you the broken balcony again
and the sky-dog
that held rain in the well

I shall find for you the same soldiers again
he who vanished three years ago
with a hole above his eye
and he who knocked on doors at night
with amputated hand

I shall find for you the rotten apple again

Do not go away beast
beast with the iron teeth

EXPERIMENTS FOR THE REPETITION OF NIGHT

My friends are leaving
they have come to say goodbye

I shall never see my friends again

one of them is leaving for the adjacent room
his face turned black
he wore a dark green material
night has fallen
he no longer speaks

the other is leaving for the other room
to find pins
first however he hid himself behind the curtains
he became frightened
afterwards he climbed on the window
to sleep

the other took off his shoes
with trembling hands
he took them to warm
the statue
he took it into the bedroom
he does not know how to make it stand upright

my friends have gone far away

I shall not see my friends
again

THE SCENE

On the table they had placed upright
a head of clay
they had decorated their walls
with flowers
on the bed they had cut out of paper
two erotic bodies
on the floor snakes scurried
and butterflies
a huge dog kept guard
in the corner

Strings stretched across the room
from all sides
it would be imprudent for anyone
to pull them
one of the strings pushed the bodies
to make love

The unhappiness outside
clawed the doors

THE TELEPHONE

We telephone
for a dead man
where can we find him?
His name?
they reply
He has no name
he is dead
we search
the drawers
They have hidden him
They have chased him away
They have saved him
we can't find him
he is dead
they tell us to run
in the rain
to find him
we run
and do not find him
I telephone
and they tell me He has gone
they must be lying
I see HER
with my large eye
the crimson one
Let's go elsewhere
to wander about
and to ask
They don't know her

They don't know his name
They've forgotten him
I telephone
they tell me: No
They don't know who I am
They don't know my name
They've forgotten me

I am dead

NOSTALGIA RETURNS

The woman undressed and lay on the bed
a kiss opened and closed on the floor
savage shapes with knives began to appear on the ceiling
hung on a wall, a bird choked and vanished
a candle leant and fell from its holder
weeping was heard outside and the clatter of feet

The windows opened a hand entered
afterwards the moon entered
embraced the woman and they slept together
All night long a voice was heard:

The days pass
the snow remains

THE CARNIVAL

This carnival took place far away in another world
the small hobbyhorse wandered in the desolate streets
where not a soul was breathing
dead children were continually rising into the sky
they would descend for a moment
to get the paper kites they had left behind
snow fell like glass confetti
and wounded every heart
a kneeling woman
turned up her eyes as though she were dead
only troops of soldiers passed by one-two
one-two with frozen teeth

At night the moon appeared
a carnival moon
filled with hate
they bound it and cast it into the sea
knifed

This carnival took place far away
in another world

THE DOVE

The dove was to pass this way
they had lit torches on all the roads
other men kept guard by rows of trees
children held small flags in their hands
the hours passed and it began to rain
afterwards all the sky darkened
a lightning flash whispered something fearfully
and the outcry opened in the mouth of men

then the white dove with savage teeth
howled like a dog in the night

MARIA

Maria was pensively
taking off her stockings

Out of her body
voices rose of other human beings
that of a soldier who spoke like a bird
that of a sick man who had died from sheep pains
and the weeping of a small niece of Maria's
who in these past few days had just been born

Maria wept and wept
now Maria laughed
at night she spread out her hands
with her legs wide open

Afterwards her eyes darkened
black black opaque they darkened

The radio played
Maria wept
Maria wept
The radio played

Then Maria
slowly slowly opened her arms
and began to fly
round and round the room

THE TEMPTATION

Behind the old women dressed in black
behind their backs
is the white bed
and on it all by itself the apple
just as even before the apple
the white flower was all by itself
they tore it with knives with scissors
they watered it with blood
and now on the bed
a rotted apple lies

this is why the angel sits by the edge of the bed
behind the old ladies dressed in black
behind their backs
he opens his white wings
and stretches his hand toward the apple

LIFE

Night
in a pharmacy
a kneeling
horse
eats
the floorboards
a girl
with a strange
green
burn
is being healed
while the ghost
in despair
weeps
in the corner

PENTAGRAM

Limned mouths
the fire entered
the smoke
smashed your teeth

a girl
burned her dress
because she was freezing
she says I love frozen garments
and I hold only one flower for you
thank you

a beggar
says Do you know what?
a father has become
a pistol
but I
have a large room
with red curtains
go away!
you are not men
you are moons
I never want to see you again!

a man
searches
the streets
picks up pieces
of paper
cigarette boxes
smiles
and says I am a murderer
what else?

and I
heavy of heart
annihilated
in difficult times
together with these
burst in a white death
with blood

THE MORNING AND THE EVENING

In the morning
you see death
gazing from the window
at the garden
at the cruel bird
and the quiet cat
on the branch

outside on the road
passes the automobile ghost
the hypothetical chauffeur
the man with the broom
the golden teeth
he laughs
and in the evening
at the movies
you see
whatever you did not see in the morning
the joyful gardener
the real automobile
kisses with a real couple

you see that the movies
do not love death

THE STATION

In memory of Guillaume Apollinaire

In my sleep it is always raining
my dreams fill with mud
there is a dark landscape
and I am waiting for a train
the stationmaster gathers daisies
which have sprouted amid the rails
because no train has come
to this station for a long time
and the years have suddenly passed
I sit behind a windowpane
my hair and beard have grown long
as though I were very ill
and as sleep once more takes me
she comes slowly slowly
she holds a knife in her hands
she approaches me carefully
and plunges the knife in my right eye

THE MONEY

The gypsy woman says
I read money
in your dream
you will have a crowded life
filled with snow
but I do not know
when you will pass on

the shepherd says
When you do not love the stars
my sheep will hate you
and I shall give you
that half of the moon
which vomits flame from the side of rage

death says
The money is mine
the moon also is mine
the snow and the sheep are mine
and the red flames
and
the gypsy woman
and
the shepherd

ONE DAY

The eyelashes of day have become blear-eyed
a girl hangs over the windowsill like a flower
though around her the birds sing passionately
a shattered cup
with its splinters invisible in the heart
and a paper kite high up like a rebellious dream
emits flame
we gather needles
as in another time they gathered flowers
and the largest of the needles
pierces through our skull

THE DESOLATE

Desolate men in the cold
speak to the Virgin

Without expression
without leaves
the tree stares at them

ravens have dressed in red
like whores

the church has cracked
from too much rain
the saints were found
running in the streets

THE MIRROR

When my mirror had returned
to the sky
a moon half-eaten
by the red ants of fire
appeared
with a head beside it
also burning within a fiery rain
the head glittered
and glowed
and whispered
as the fire took it and turned it to coal:
The trees burn and disappear like hair
the angel vanishes with singed wings
and pain
a dog with broken leg
remains
remains

I WIN

Every night
a black veil falls
which the sun burns
at night
the moon stains it with blood
every night I win I win
my death
stretches out its hand
every night I win I win

THE GOLD

Sometime
we shall stop
like a blue carriage
amid the gold

we shall not count the black horses
we shall have nothing to add up
we shall no longer have anything
to divide

holding
a stick
we shall pass through the black burning hole
of the sun

THE POET

When they find me on the wooden slab of my death
the sky will have turned red from end to end
there will be the slightest suspicion of sea
and a white bird from above in a now
frightening darkness will recite my songs

BENJAMIN

When Benjamin awoke and heard
the birds warbling
We also had—he said—a bird in a cage
let's go now and see what's become of it.
He went and the cage was a black bowl
in which a small goldfish was burning
It's still in flames—he said—I thought it had burned down
many years ago

SUNDAY

My eyes are Sunday waves
my hands are waves of loneliness

the teeth in my heart
grind in an innocent sleep

the dead child
does not live abroad
it walks on holding a red puppy
in a handkerchief

monsters walk
upside down in dreams
a fierce wind is blowing
above the lemonades
a bat flies
like a sorrowful gospel

with a black cloth
a woman covers
the moon

THRENODY

Girls like torn cardboard
with stains of sulphur in their heads
with wrathful weeds in their heads
smashing the cup of the sky
with tears straining in their eyes
like black brand-new pins
when will the color of birds sing?
when will butterflies strike at knives?
when other hands will sprout on suns
and sleep will drain them of darkness

and night shall be as beautiful as day

*

*This book was composed on the Linotype
in Electra and printed by
Theo. Gaus' Sons, Inc., Brooklyn, N.Y. 11201*